# Preserving Smithville

*Building memories one picture at a time*

Written and photographed by Barbara A. Fanson

Published by Sterling Education Centre Inc.

Thank you for reading.
If you have a moment, please post a review on Amazon.

For other books by the same author:

http://fanson.net

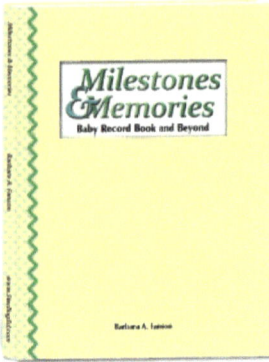

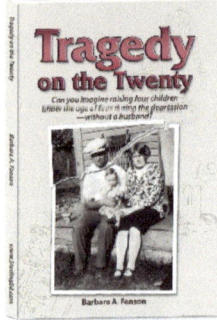

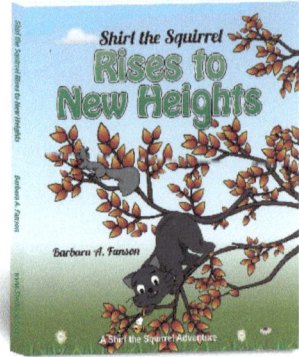

**Other books by Barbara Fanson:**

*Tragedy on the Twenty,* a historical fiction about an accident on Hwy. 20 in 1933 published by Sterling Education Centre.

*Milestones & Memories,* a baby record book and beyond, published by Sterling Education Centre.

*Shirl the Squirrel Rises to New Heights*, a children's picture book published by Sterling Education Centre.

*Start & Run a Desktop Publishing Business,* published by Self-Counsel Press.

*Producing a First-Class Newsletter*, published by Self-Counsel Press.

# Preserving Smithville
### *Building memories on picture at a time*

**Sterling Education Centre Inc.**
220 Homebrook Drive, Mount Hope, ON L0R 1W0
Email: learn@sterlinged.com        Phone: (905) 679-9229

# Contents

This book is dedicated to all the people
who have painted, renovated, and maintained
their homes.

Thank you for sharing your house with us.

A special thanks to Bev Carruthers
who manages the Memories of Smithville Facebook page
and to the West Lincoln Historical Society
for preserving information about the area.

# Smithville, Ontario
## *The Heart of the Niagara Peninsula*

Smithville is located between Hamilton and St. Catharines in the middle of the Niagara Peninsula. In 1787, Richard Griffin, his wife Mary (nee Smith) and their children were United Empire Loyalists who came to the Smithville from Nine Partners, New York. The sons were Abraham, Edward, Nathaniel, Isaiah, Smith, Jonathan, and Richard Jr. The family occupied lots 6 to 12 on Concession 9 by Twenty Mile Creek in Grimsby Township. They called this settlement Griffintown, but later renamed it after Richard's wife Mary Griffin, whose maiden name was Smith.

Son Edward (Ned) Griffin thought he was the real founder of the village because he chopped the first tree, chose the site, cleared the first acre of land, built the first house, and stayed his entire life in the village.

Son Smith Griffin built a tread wheel in 1810 so settlers could ground their grain. Later he built a dam and mill on Twenty Mile Creek. He also started an ashery.

Son Edward Griffin opened a general store.

By 1849, Smithville had a population of 150 and were granted a post office for delivery twice a week. By now, there was a grist mill, saw mill, carding machine, cloth factory, four stores, machine shop, tannery, two blacksmiths, two tailors, and two shoemakers.

By the 1950s Smithville had a population of almost 1,000 people.

On Jan. 1, 1970, Smithville and South Grimsby Township amalgamated into the Township of West Lincoln.

---

**Edwardian-style house**

Gable
*(with scalloped shingles)*

Brackets

Cornice Return

Doric Column

In 1997, I renovated this Edwardian-style house with large gables, brackets under the roof, cornice returns, and 10 Doric columns, which took 9 hours to strip, sand, and repaint each one. It was built in 1913.
—*Author Barbara A. Fanson*

**This monument is erected on Griffin Street:**

In grateful memory of
Edward Griffin and his descendants
Born ... 1764  Died April 13, 1863
Second son of
Richard Griffin and Mary Smith
He came to Canada in 1786
And settled on the site of
The present village of Smithville
This tablet was erected by
Members of the Griffin Clan.

The Smithville Railway Station was built in 1903 for the TH&B (Toronto, Hamilton & Buffalo) railway company. Located at 288 Station Street in Smithville.

The Train station has a tower, which starts at ground level. A turret is a smaller tower attached to a structure, usually a corner or angle. Notice the finial at the top of the witch's hat, I mean roof.

Built in 1903, TH&B (Toronto, Hamilton, & Buffalo) Train Station houses the West Lincoln Historical Society. You can go in and see archives—or better yet—volunteer. Check their website for days the archives are open to the public.

The Smithville train station is also home to the West Lincoln Chamber of Commerce. In the early 1900's, the Smithville Board of Trade was formed; today it is the West Lincoln Chamber of Commerce.

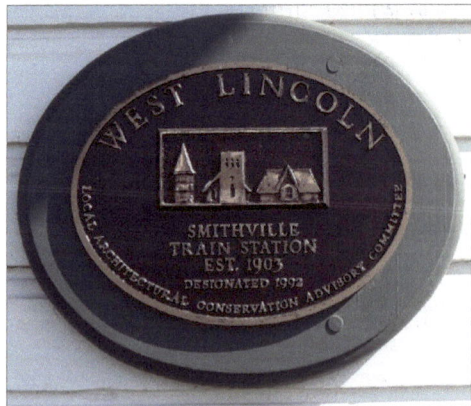

The Merritt Funeral Home was established in 1921 and located at 287 Station Street since 1926. They are celebrating over 97 years with four generations. 2-story pillars support a large pediment with brackets under the roof.

279 Station Street has a hipped roof, dormer on the roof, pediment—the triangle on the roof of the porch, and four Doric columns supporting the porch roof.

Formerly CIL Fertilizer, this industrial style building at 270 Station Street houses Lou Stranges & Associates accounting and office supplies, as well as Deliveries Unlimited.

233 Station St. features a big bay window with brackets under the roof of the bay window. Notice they have a front gable and a side gable.

The Smithville Church of Christ is located at 246 Station Street and has lancet windows: long, narrow windows with a point at the top.

St. Luke's Anglican Church at 216 Station Street has buttresses supporting the sides of the church and arched windows and doors.

In the heart of Smithville, 204 Station Street features a bay window with arch window frames, gables, and dormer with window at the front of the house above the porch.

Griffin Street at Station Street in 1981. Both buildings and Central Motors are gone and replaced by Angelo's House of Hair. Notice the recessed entrance on the white building, which was common in retail buildings of this period. Both buildings have a false front but a gabled roof behind.

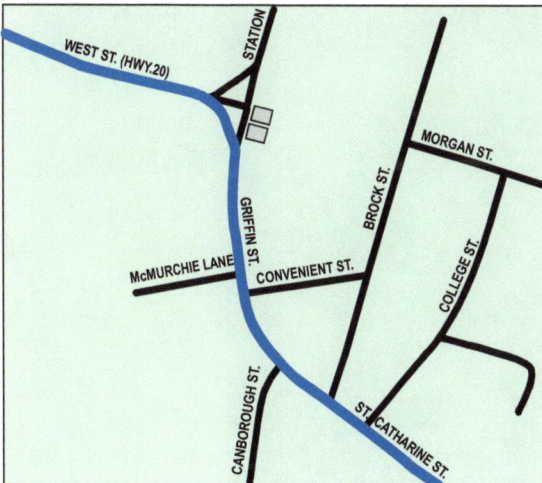

College Street Public School was at 132 College Street but it moved to where South Lincoln High School was at 260 Canborough Street. It is now called Smithville Public School.

The roof with the segmental dormer window is the oldest part of the school, which used to be Smithville High School.

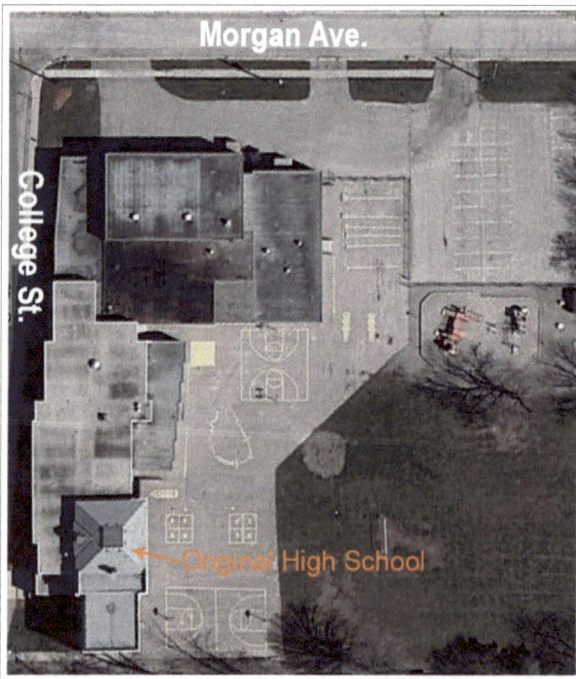

Sometimes, a segmental dormer is called an arch dormer.

Look at the aerial view to see all the building additions.

136 Brock Street features a large bay window jutting out from a wall.

The Greek Community Centre is located on West St.

Notice the arched door, fancy woodwork at the top of the shutters, and stonework at 271 West Street. It also has cornice returns, a decorative element on the end of the two gables (peaks).

This classic, well-maintained home at 265 West Street has a dormer on the roof, a large bay window, and lead glass in the door.

249 West Street has a Gothic Revival style because of the peak in the roof and it has a rounded upper window. Notice the elaborately carved verge boards attached to the peak.

238 West St is a Tudor Revival style house with unique arched door. Notice the stonework was continued at the base of the chimney and on the lower corner of the house.

Currently Rolly's Smokehouse, some will remember this building at 214 West Street as the Old Farm Inn or Shep's Inn. It has three dormers and a unique roof.

The Tudor Revival house at 135 West Street has a unique window on the left.

"Dr. Bond's House" is one of the most distinctive houses in Smithville—and the hardest to photograph because of the healthy shade trees in the front yard! Although the Bond family has not lived here in decades, many will remember visiting the doctor in this house.

Did you notice the large brackets under the right window and the gable with three windows jutting out of the sloped roof? This house also has a large dormer at the front.

There aren't many houses in Smithville with a stone porch, though Grimsby has many.

Notice the Palladian windows on the top floor of 121 West Street—the middle window is bigger than the other two. It also has a lovely wraparound porch and arched windows.

Although the façade has been changed, 115 West Street is an Edwardian style house with a hipped roof (four sides with a peak), a dormer sticking out of the roof, and curved arches above the second-story windows.

*Preserving Smithville*

St. Martin Catholic School was located at 186 Margaret Street, but a new school opened in 2017 at 18 Streamside Drive, near Regional Road 20.

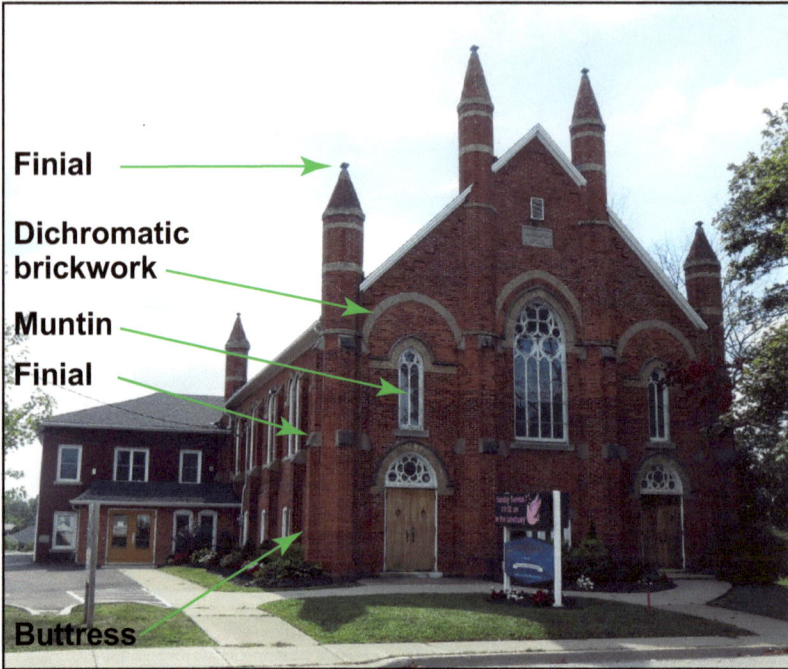

Finial

Dichromatic brickwork

Muntin

Finial

Buttress

The Smithville United Church is located at 116 West Street, Started in 1791 as the Methodist Episcopal Church, they celebrated 225 years in 2016.

The church was built in 1882 with a Gothic Revival style including buttresses decorated with finials, dichromatic brickwork, and muntins in the windows.

**Buttress:** a masonry structure built against a wall or projecting from a wall, which helps support, the wall or reinforce it.

**Dichromatic brickwork:** the use of two colours of brick, tile, or slate to decorate a wall.

**Finial:** (or decorative feature) is an element at the top of an object for decoration. Often carved in stone, a finial emphasizes the apex of a dome, spire, tower, roof, or gable.

**Muntins**: When a window has more that one glass pane, the material separating the panes is called a muntin. In a stained glass window, each coloured piece of glass is held in place with a muntin.

This Edwardian house at 197 Griffin Street has a dormer on the hipped roof where all four sides slope down to the walls. This building also has several lead glass windows and brackets under the front porch roof.

195 Griffin Street has had several businesses over the years including Book Funeral Home, Willy's Flowers, and now Vitality Smithville. Notice the semi-round tower on the side.

Did you notice the wooden brackets under the roof and the big bay window at 159 Griffin Street? This house looks square with a lot of attachments and details added.

Remember when you could park out front and run into Service Cleaners or Nichol's Drugstore? Today, True Men's Barber Shop and Royal LePage occupy 111 & 107 Griffin St.

The left building was built in 1830 as a post office by Smith Griffin, later the Service Cleaners, and now True Men's Barber Shop. Notice the brickwork on the right building.

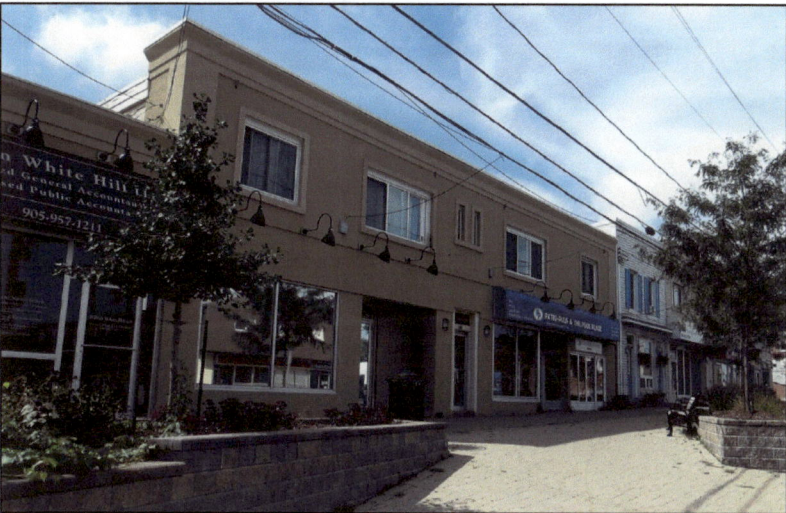

Gone are the post office, Sammy Magder's General Dry Goods, Quality Bakery, 5¢ to $1 Store, and Boulter's Meats. Updated and replaced. Now the Post Office is in the Village Square on St. Catharines Street and Industrial Road.

Do you remember when this clock hung in front of the post office, which became the Service Cleaners? You could see the clock from the bridge over Twenty Mile Creek.

The clock was hung in February of 1939 at the Post Office at 111 Griffin St.

It was removed in 2004, when the clock face was damaged. Now it hangs in the Murgatroyd Parkette at the corner of St. Catherine St. and Griffin St.

If you look closely at the clock, you can see "In Memory of Jacob W. Roy." It was a gift given in memory of the late Jacob M. Roy by his daughter, Sarah Correvon. Roy was one of Smithville's first residents and entrepreneurs, who owned several businesses in town. The

West Lincoln Historical Archives lists Jacob M. Roy as a farmer, asher (dealing with ashes), labourer, and businessman.

Jacob M. Roy was born in 1824 in Smithville, Ontario, Canada, son of Stephen Roy and Lydia Roszel. He married Elizabeth Horton in 1845 and they had 8 children.

The chicken symbol beside the clock represents "The Chicken Capital of Canada" and home of PoultryFest.

The memories of attending PoultryFest with my daughter have lasted longer than the event, which is no longer held.

Hundreds of volunteers assisted with PoultryFest, a free, one-day event. Thank you to all the volunteers who helped over the years.

How many people remember the water fountain that stood on this corner, where the Murgatroyd Parkette is now? In the 1960s, I ran to it when we walked into town.

These beautiful commercial buildings have been updated, but the brick still has original features. The left building has voussoirs—brick to form an arch—above the windows. The top, light-coloured stone is the keystone.

The building on the right was Hibbard's Hardware store where you could buy a handful of nails or Matchbox cars. Notice the brickwork with arches and recessed bricks.

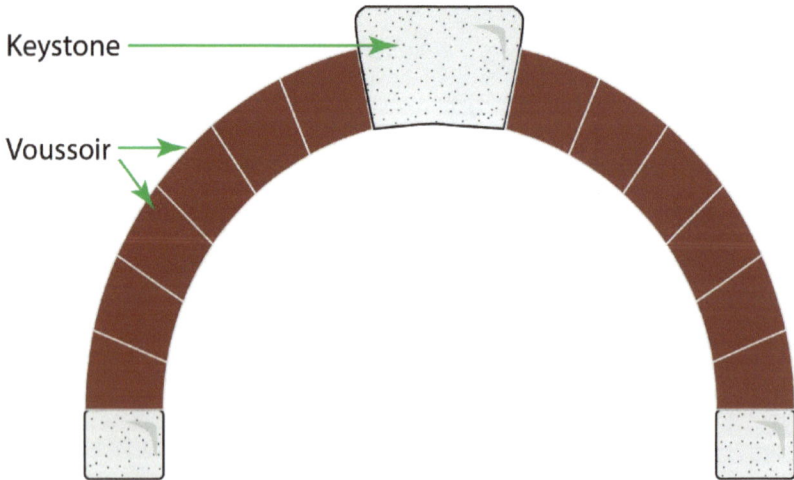

Keystone

Voussoir

Buzzard's Pizza now occupies the store that used to be the Red & White Store. The old bowling alley was upstairs. Did you notice the older home in behind X-treme PC & Electronics? It has a Palladian—3 windows with the middle one larger. 112 and 114 Griffin St.

Do you remember seeing Santa Claus in the Coronation Lodge? You probably got an orange or candy cane. It was instituted in 1911.

121 Griffin Street was once owned by the Nichol family, which owned Nichol's Drugstore. Well maintained and updated, it still has its beautiful charm.

142 Griffin Street is a simple clapboard house, but it has the decorative element on the gable.

154 Mill Street is a square house with a hep roof with four sloping sides. But it also has a shed dormer on the roof.

141 Griffin Street was a commercial building but divided into apartments.

The feed mill in Smithville is probably the oldest commercial building still standing in Smithville. Built in 1810 at 157 Griffin Street, it is next to Twenty Mile Creek.

Niagara Grain & Feed, owned by Maple Lodge Feeds, closed on May 31, 2014. The above photo was taken in the 1960s.

Originally South Lincoln High School, it is now Smithville Public School. Smithville's original high school was housed in the oldest part of what became College Street Public School. In **1954**, South Lincoln High School moved to 260 Canborough Street. The high school closed in 2017 and the students are bussed to Grimsby Secondary School or E.L. Crossley. A new school will open by Sept. 2020 elsewhere.

Barbara Fanson designed the school flag in 1978.

Notice the distinctive supports beside the windows.

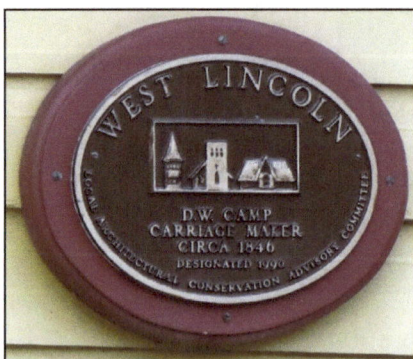

205 Canborough Street was home to D.W. Camp a carriage maker in 1846, according to the designation plaque on the wall. This cute clapboard house with a hipped roof is next to the creek.

"The Holloway House" on Canborough St. had horses in the field to the right, before the new house was built. With a large stone porch with columns, the house is also distinctive for the roof shape. It is not a mansard roof because the roof does not go down four walls. Instead, it is a gambrel roof—a two-sided roof with two slopes.

## Types of Dormers

Hipped Dormer    Shed Dormer    Gable Dormer

Eyebrow Dormer    Eyebrow Dormer    Segmental Dormer
(arched dormer)

"The Murgatroyd House" at 235 Canborough St. has had many owners and renovations over the years, but it remains a distinctive Edwardian style, popular from 1900–1930. The large gables have decorative cornice trims, but there's also a side bay window, and 12 Ionic columns with carved swirls at the top. Did you notice the Mansard roof at the back of the house?

255 Canborough Street is a classic square house, but it has a belvedere—Italian for "beautiful view"—on the roof. Some people would call it an enclosed cupola.

303 Canborough Street is a square, classic brick house with a hep roof where four sides of the roof slope down from the center. But it also has a pediment—the triangular roof above the door with columns. Notice the brackets supporting the roof of the porch.

Gothic Revival (1830-1900) is usually symmetrical with steep roof pitches and steep gables. The roof also has two shed dormers. A stone wall, large porch, and four Doric columns complete this classic and distinctive house on Canborough Street, across from the Smithville Library.

Next time you walk past 255 Canborough Street, take a look at the old water pump beside the house.

I walked past this house everyday on my way to school and admired "The House with the Mansard Roof" at 401 Canborough St. The classic white house with black trim has a Mansard roof, which is popular in France. Because the roof extends down the walls, the house doesn't require as much brick or clapboard. Notice the inverted "v" or pediment above the front door and windows? It also has several gabled dormers on the Mansard roof.

423 Canborough St. has a hipped roof and large bay windows. Notice the inverted "v" above the windows.

This Canborough St. house has side gables as well as a front gable. A Gothic Revival style house (1830-1900) is usually symmetrical with steep roof pitches and steep gables.

440 Canborough St. has a hipped roof with dormer and a large porch with simple pillars. Notice the Hurley brackets under the porch roof.

A classic Edwardian-style house with a large wraparound veranda at 462 Canborough St. The bric-a-brac on the veranda has been removed (swirled brackets).

The Presbyterian Church at 143 St. Catharine Street has a large rose window with ornamental mullions radiating from the center.  Sometimes called a Catherine window, wheel window or circular window, they are often found in churches of the Gothic architectural style.

120 St. Catharine Street is a Tudor style house with a unique arched door. Notice the stonework was continued on the chimney and on the lower corner of the house.

This Gothic Revival style house on St. Catharine Street features a symmetrical house with steep gables.

Look at the beautiful verge boards or bargeboards on the front gable of 131 St. Catharine Street.

139 St. Catharine Street is a smaller gothic revival style house.

153 St. Catharine Street is a large house with gables, bay window, and brackets under the roof of the bay window. There is a finial at the top of the gable.

The houses at 138 and 142 St. Catharine Street have similar features. They both have a pediment of three windows— with the middle one slightly bigger—on the third-floor gable.

234 St. Catharine Street is a Gothic Revival style house with two gables in the front and a dormer.

Look at the big 2-story bay window on the side of 240 St. Catharine Street.

This townhouse with 12 units was built in 1970. The address used to be 133 Townline Road, but now it's 6427 Townline Road.

The author lived in the two-story white house that used to be here and broke her arm in this tree.

The Smithville Animal Hospital at 6414 Townline Road or Smithville Road.

The Smithville Auto Parts has been gone for a long time, and now the building at 6421 Townline Road is a residential complex.

St. Matthew's Lutheran Church at 6441 Townline Road in Smithville.

Although it has been a home for several decades, this building at 9007 Highway 20 in Fulton was once a one-room schoolhouse.

## 1943 Fulton School:

**Back Row, Left to Right:** Jessie Young, Margaret Lawson, Jim MacDougall, Gord Fanson, Charlie Farrell, Bob Fanson, and Teacher Barbara Briggs.

**Middle Row, Left to Right:** Alex MacDougall, Lorne Nelson, Lorne Young, Harry Fanson, Rod Jacobs, Lorna Cole, and Donna Nelson.

**Front Row, Left to Right:** Carman Stirling, Don Jackson, Ann Ogibowski, Barbara Jackson, Joan Lawson, Betty Lawson, and Jean Bortolotto.

## 1946 Fulton School, S.S. #9, South Grimsby:

**Back Row, Left to Right:** _____, _____, Charlie Farrell, Alex McDougall, Jessie Young, Teacher Marie Thomas, Bob Fanson, Lorne Nelson, and Harry Fanson.

**Front Row, Left to Right:** _____, _____, _____, _____, _____, Lorna Cole, Donna Nelson, John Jackson, and _____.

Janetta Fanson had this house built in 1933 next to the Fulton Store in Fulton. The photo above was taken in 2001.

This is the same house at 9004 on Highway 20 in Fulton, taken in 2018, but the porch and siding have changed.

Janetta Fanson outside the house in 1951. Notice the front porch has changed several times since it was built in 1933.

You can see the Fulton Garage in the background.

Janetta Fanson's sons Gordon, Harry, Robert, and Orval stand on the front yard of their house with the Fulton Store and a single gas pump in the background.

This ad for Sam Magder's General Dry Goods ran in the 1957 Cives Futuri yearbook for South Lincoln High School.

2001 photo of the Fulton Store, which has changed many times over the years. Today, it is Fulton Subs & Convenience at 9003 Regional Road, Smithville.

This ad for Lorne Killins and Son's Red & White Store ran in the 1957 Cives Futuri yearbook for South Lincoln High School. Notice the telephone number and no street address.

These ads appeared in the 1957 Cives Futuri yearbook for South Lincoln High School. There's no street address and the telephone number for Shep's Inn is 8 and Merritt's Funeral Home is 40.

Thank you for reading.

If you have a moment, please post a review on Amazon.ca

For other books by the same author:

http://fanson.net